**W9-CHR-735**

796.357   St. Sauver, Dennis
SAI   New York Mets

DATE DUE			

MLB's Greatest Teams

NEW YORK METS

Big Buddy Books

An Imprint of Abdo Publishing
abdobooks.com

Dennis St. Sauver

abdobooks.com

Published by Abdo Publishing, a division of ABDO, PO Box 398166, Minneapolis, Minnesota 55439.
Copyright © 2019 by Abdo Consulting Group, Inc. International copyrights reserved in all countries. No part
of this book may be reproduced in any form without written permission from the publisher. Big Buddy Books™
is a trademark and logo of Abdo Publishing.

Printed in the United States of America, North Mankato, Minnesota.
102018
012019

THIS BOOK CONTAINS
RECYCLED MATERIALS

Cover Photo: Elsa/Getty Images.
Interior Photos: 33ft/Depositphotos (p. 7); AP Images (pp. 15, 19, 22); Dave Pickoff/AP Images (p. 28);
    Fernando Medina/Getty Images (p. 23); Harry How/Getty Images (p. 27); Jim Wells/AP Images (p. 13);
    John J. Lent/AP Images (p. 11); Kevin C. Cox/Getty Images (pp. 23, 24, 25); Mark Brown/Getty Images
    (p. 24); Mike Ehrmann/Getty Images (p. 5); Mike Stobe/Getty Images (p. 9); Paul Benoit/AP Images (p.
    21); Ray Stubblebine/AP Images (p. 17); Rich Schultz/Getty Images (p. 29).

Coordinating Series Editor: Tamara L. Britton
Contributing Series Editor: Jill M. Roesler
Graphic Design: Jenny Christensen, Cody Laberda

Library of Congress Control Number: 2018948455

Publisher's Cataloging-in-Publication Data

Names: St. Sauver, Dennis, author.
Title: New York Mets / by Dennis St. Sauver.
Description: Minneapolis, Minnesota : Abdo Publishing, 2019 | Series: MLB's
    greatest teams set 2 | Includes online resources and index.
Identifiers: ISBN 9781532118111 (lib. bdg.) | ISBN 9781532171154 (ebook)
Subjects: LCSH: New York Mets (Baseball team)--Juvenile literature. | Baseball
    teams--United States--History--Juvenile literature. | Major League Baseball
    (Organization)--Juvenile literature. | Baseball--Juvenile literature.
Classification: DDC 796.35764--dc23

Contents

Major League Baseball

League Pla...

There are two leagues in MLB. They the American League (AL) National League (NL). Each has 15 teams and is sp... three divisions. The are east, central, and west.

The New York Mets is one of 30 Major League Baseball (MLB) teams. The team plays in the National League East **Division**.

Throughout the season, all MLB teams play 162 games. The season begins in April and can continue until November.

Mr. Met is the team's mascot. He was named America's Favorite Mascot in 2012. His partner mascot is Mrs. Met.

A Winning Team

The Mets team is from Queens, New York. The team's colors are blue, orange, and white.

The team has had good seasons and bad. But time and again, the Mets players have proven themselves. Let's see what makes the Mets one of MLB's greatest teams!

Fast Facts

HOME FIELD: Citi Field

TEAM COLORS: Blue, orange, and white

TEAM SONG: "Meet The Mets" by Ruth Roberts and Bill Katz

PENNANTS: 5

WORLD SERIES TITLES: 1969, 1986

6

CANADA

UNITED STATES
OF AMERICA

MEXICO

N
W   E
S

CANADA

LAKE ONTARIO

New York

Vermont

Massachusetts

Pennsylvania

Connecticut

Queens

New
Jersey

ATLANTIC
OCEAN

Citi Field

The Mets' first game was held at the Polo Grounds in 1962. They played there for only two years before moving to Shea Stadium. The Mets played at Shea Stadium for 44 years!

In 2009, the Mets moved into the open-air stadium called Citi Field. It holds nearly 42,000 fans. Citi Field is sometimes used for concerts and other sports events.

In its first year, the Mets had only 40 wins and 120 losses. That was the team's worst year on record.

Then and Now

The Mets began in 1962 as one of two new teams added to the NL. The team struggled with losing records for seven years.

Then in 1969, the team surprised everyone in baseball. It had its first successful season by winning 100 games. The Mets went on to win the World Series that year!

The New York Mets played a 23-inning baseball game in 1964. At seven hours and 23 minutes, it is the second-longest game in MLB history.

Players continued their winning ways for the next few years. In 1973, they won the NL **Championship** Series. The team went to the World Series again that year. But they lost this time four games to three.

One of the greatest goals for all teams is to make it to the World Series. The Mets have been there five times and won twice.

The Mets began using a "Bullpen Buggy" during the 1970s.
The baseball-shaped cart drove pitchers to the mound.

Highlights

The Mets had won the 1969 World Series and the 1973 **pennant**. Sadly, the team experienced losing seasons from 1977 to 1983.

But the team **rebounded** quickly. The Mets had winning seasons again for the next seven years. And the players went to the **playoffs** twice during that time.

Hall of Famer Willie Mays got his very last hit with the Mets. It was during the 1973 World Series.

The top team from each AL and NL division goes to the playoffs. Each league also sends one wild-card team. One team from the AL and one from the NL will win the pennant. The two pennant winners then go to the World Series!

In 1986, the Mets won its second World Series. And in the following three decades, the team posted 17 winning seasons!

Players went to the World Series again in 2000 and 2015. Sadly, they lost both times. But the Mets team remains highly respected and well-loved by its fans.

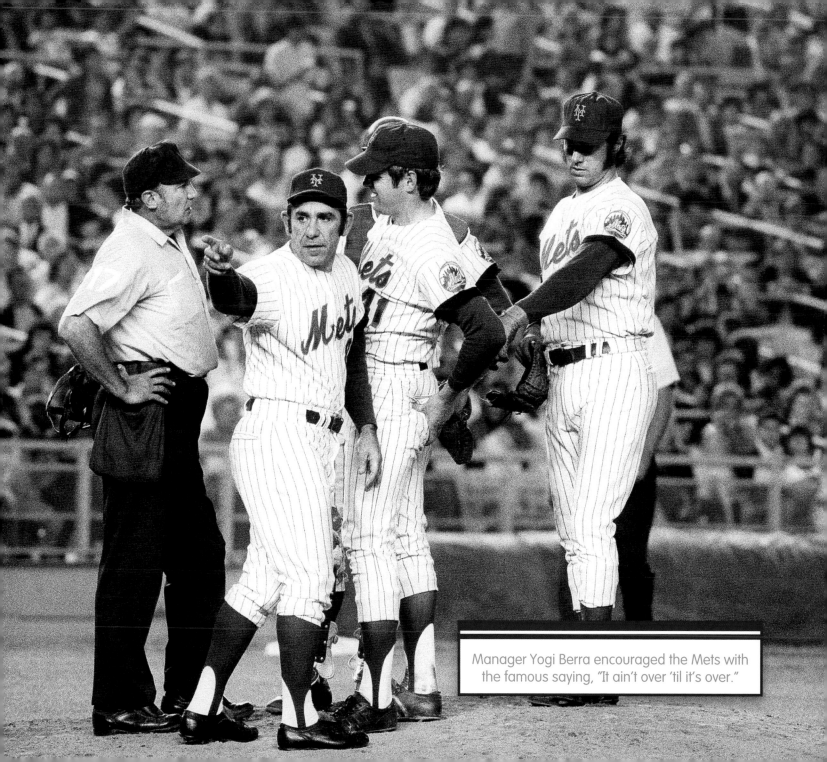

Manager Yogi Berra encouraged the Mets with the famous saying, "It ain't over 'til it's over."

Famous Managers

Gil Hodges was the Mets' original first baseman in 1962. He hit the first-ever home run in Mets history during the team's first game.

In 1968, he became the team's **skipper**. The very next year, Hodges led the team to a World Series victory! And he helped the Mets to winning records over the next three years.

Sadly, Hodges died suddenly in 1972. His loss was felt by Mets fans everywhere.

The 1969 team was called The Miracle Mets. That is because no one expected the team to win the World Series.

Davey Johnson is thought to be the best manager that the Mets ever had. He managed from 1984 to 1990. During this time, the Mets never finished below second place in its **division**.

Under Johnson's management, the team won two division titles and a World Series. Many think the Mets were the strongest NL team while Johnson was manager.

Johnson won a Manager of the Year Award in both the AL and the NL!

Star Players

Tom Seaver PITCHER, #41

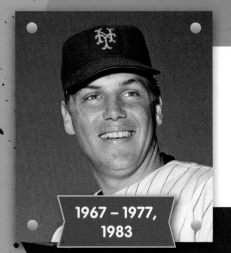

1967 – 1977, 1983

Tom Seaver was a star pitcher for the Mets. He won the 1967 **Rookie** of the Year Award. Two years later, he helped the Mets win the World Series. Seaver earned the Cy Young Award for best pitcher three different times. In 1992, he was **inducted** to the National Baseball Hall of Fame.

Dwight Gooden PITCHER, #16

Dwight Gooden was just 19 when he won the Rookie of the Year Award. In 1985, he won 24 games and the Cy Young Award. That year he also earned the NL Pitcher of the Year Award. Many knew Dwight for his fastball, which he often threw at 98 miles (158 km) per hour!

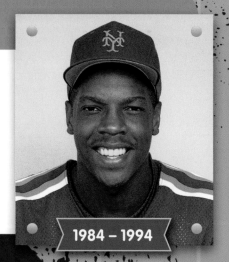

1984 – 1994

Mike Piazza CATCHER AND FIRST BASEMAN, #31

Mike Piazza joined the Mets in the 1998 season. He was a very powerful hitter. He won ten **Silver Slugger Awards** during his successful **career**. Throughout his career, he hit 396 homers as a catcher. And 220 of those he hit while playing for the Mets. Piazza still holds the MLB record for catcher with the most home runs.

1998 – 2005

José Reyes SHORTSTOP, #7

José Reyes helped lead the Mets to the NL **Championship** Series in 2006. Reyes was a four-time All-Star. In 2011, he won the NL batting title. He was one of the best Mets **lead-off hitters**. Reyes played for three other teams from 2012 to 2015. But he came back to the Mets in 2016.

2003 – 2011, 2016 –

David Wright THIRD BASEMAN, #5

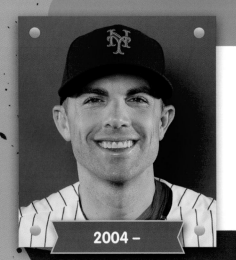

2004 –

David Wright has spent his entire career with the Mets. Teammates call him "Captain America." That is because he is the captain of the team. Wright has made the NL All-Star team seven times. He has also earned two Silver Slugger Awards for batting. And he won two Gold Gloves for fielding.

Jacob deGrom PITCHER, #48

In 2014, Jacob deGrom earned the NL Rookie of the Year Award. Later he pitched for the team during the 2015 playoffs. That year, he helped the team win the division title and the NL pennant. In 2016, deGrom pitched a shutout game. That means he did not allow any of the other team's batters to score.

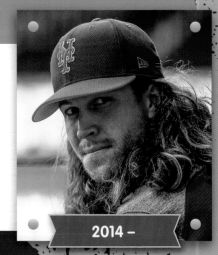

2014 –

Yoenis Céspedes OUTFIELDER, #52

Yoenis Céspedes was born in Cuba. He is a powerful slugger for the Mets. Céspedes won the MLB Home Run Derby Contest in both 2013 and 2014. In only four years with the Mets, Céspedes hit 73 homers! And he has been selected for the NL All-Star team two times. In 2016, he earned his first NL **Silver Slugger Award**.

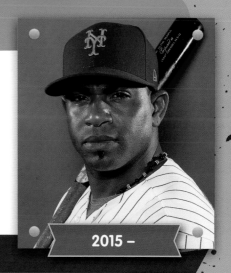

2015 –

AJ Ramos PITCHER, #44

AJ's full name is Alejandro Ramos. He joined the team in 2017. Before the Mets, he was a **closing pitcher** for the Miami Marlins. In 2016, Ramos was named to the NL All-Star team. The next year, his pitching saved 27 games for the Mets!

2017 –

25

Final Call

The Mets have a long, rich history. The team has played in five World Series, and earned two World Series titles.

Even during losing seasons, true fans have stuck by the players. Many believe the Mets will remain one of the greatest teams in MLB.

In 2018, Jacob deGrom was the starting pitcher for 25 straight games. In those games, fewer than four players scored a run on his pitches. This tied an MLB record.

Through the Years

1964

The team **celebrated** opening day in the new Shea Stadium in New York. Sadly, they lost to the Pittsburgh Pirates in front of nearly 50,000 fans.

→

1969

The Mets played in what became known as the Black Cat Game. A black cat crossed in front of the Chicago Cubs' **dugout** during a game. The Mets won that game and went on to win the World Series!

1973

Players beat the Cincinnati Reds to win the NL **Championship** Series.

1986

The Mets won its second World Series title after beating the Boston Red Sox.

28

1999

Mets player Robin Ventura became the first MLB player to hit a homer in both games of a **doubleheader**.

2000

The team won seven to zero in Game Five of the NL **Championship** Series. The Mets went to the World Series!

2002

Mets player José Reyes hit 2,000 pitches as an MLB batter.

2017

The Mets hired Cleveland Indians' pitching coach Mickey Callaway. He is the twenty-first Mets manager. Many expect that he will help the New York team win.

Glossary

captain the leader of a team.

career a period of time spent in a certain job.

celebrate to observe a holiday or important occasion with special events.

championship a game, a match, or a race held to find a first-place winner.

closing pitcher a pitcher who gets the final outs in a game when his team is in the lead.

division a number of teams grouped together in a sport for competitive purposes.

doubleheader two games played one right after the other on the same day.

dugout a low shelter facing a baseball diamond and containing the players' bench.

Gold Glove Award annually given to the MLB players with the best fielding experience.

induct to officially introduce someone as a member.

lead-off hitter the batter who bats first in the team's lineup.

pennant the prize that is awarded to the champions of the two MLB leagues each year.

playoffs a game or series of games to determine a championship or break a tie.

rebound the act of bouncing back after hitting something.

rookie a player who is new to the major leagues until he meets certain criteria.

Silver Slugger Award given every year to the best offensive players in MLB.

skipper a person who leads or manages a team.

Online Resources

Booklinks
NONFICTION NETWORK
FREE! ONLINE NONFICTION RESOURCES

31

To learn more about the New York Mets, visit **abdobooklinks.com**. These links are routinely monitored and updated to provide the most current information available.

Index